THE ENVIRONMENT & HEALTH

Brian R. Ward

Series consultant:
Dr Alan Maryon-Davis
MB, BChir, MSc, MRCP, FFCM

LIFE GUIDES

Franklin Watts
London · New York · Toronto · Sydney

© 1989 Franklin Watts

First published in 1989 by
Franklin Watts
12a Golden Square
London W1

First published in the USA by
Franklin Watts Inc.
387 Park Avenue South
New York, N.Y. 10016

First published in Australia by
Franklin Watts Australia
14 Mars Road
Lane Cove
New South Wales 2066

UK ISBN: 0 86313 7318
US ISBN: 0-531-10644-6
Library of Congress Catalog Card No: 88-50364

Design: Howard Dyke

Picture research: Fiona Purvis

Illustrations: Dick Bonson, Penny Dann,
Howard Dyke, David Mallott

Photographs:

John Clear 33*b*
Howard Dyke/Mike Newton 23, 25*b*, 36*t*
Sally & Richard Greenhill 11*t*, 32, 42
Hutchison Library 34, 35
Robert Harding 25*t*, 28, 39
Magnum photo 26
Network 15, 17, 33*t*, 40, 41
Science Photo Library 11*b*, 12
Thames Water 18
John Watney 29
Zefa 5, 6, 9, 10, 20, 43, 45

Printed in Belgium

Contents

Introduction

The environment includes our homes, the areas in which we live and work, the air we breathe, and other conditions such as unemployment, schooling and family life.

Sometimes the environment has a direct effect on our physical health, and can be a factor in some types of disease. It can also have an effect on our emotional health, and a bad environment is thought to be responsible for much depression and anxiety. But the environment can also have positive effects on health, and a good environment at home, at school or at work all contribute towards feeling healthy and happy.

Many environmental problems which threaten health are outside an individual's control. Pollution and possible threats from nuclear weapons or power stations, for example, are problems that only governments can resolve. But you can have an influence on these problems. You can make your feelings known through one of the many organizations which exist to help protect the environment. The addresses of some of these groups are given on page 44.

Opposite
Children playing in ordinary back streets can be at risk from their environment in all sort of ways. Even the air they breathe can be contaminated by factory wastes or fumes from car exhausts. We cannot escape the environment we live in, even when it causes health problems.

4

The air we breathe

In Tokyo, where the problem of air pollution is particularly severe, many people wear smog masks to filter out the worst of its effects. However, these masks cannot remove the smallest particles and irritating gases which can damage health.

Because the air we breathe is invisible, it is difficult to think of it as a possible risk to health. Yet because of the tremendous amount of air which passes in and out of our lungs every day, even small amounts of air pollution can eventually cause health problems. The nostrils and trachea are very efficient at cleaning the air we breathe and filtering out particles of dust and soot but sometimes, pollutants damage the cleaning mechanism or are still present in large amounts when they reach the lungs.

Throughout the world, lung diseases like **bronchitis** can occur wherever factories and power stations discharge smoke into the atmosphere. If the smoke cannot easily blow away, as happens in some sheltered valleys, then air pollution builds up and the health risk is increased.

Although most people think of air pollution as being an industrial problem, many of us suffer from the effects of a form of natural pollution. In spring and summer, huge amounts of microscopic pollen grains are blown in the wind. When these are inhaled, they can cause **hay fever**.

The air we breathe contains many forms of contamination, like tiny particles of dust, soot and pollen, all of which can collect in the lungs and can cause inflammation. The lungs normally clean themselves of this material, when tiny, beating hairs called **cilia** pump a stream of sticky **mucus** up out of the lungs, carrying the trapped dirt with it. But some substances in smoke paralyze these beating cilia, so dirt and mucus accumulate, causing an irritating cough and sometimes leading to lung infection.

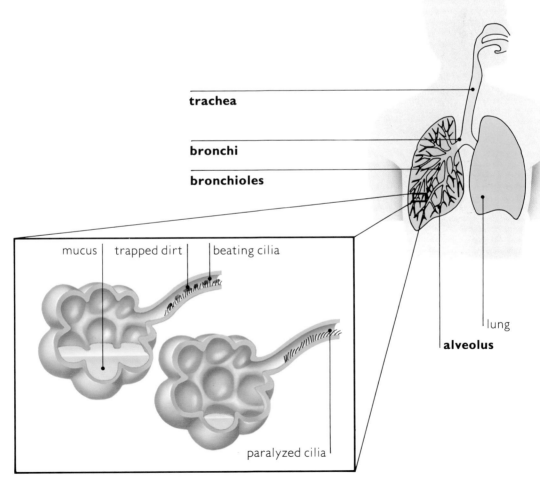

trachea

bronchi

bronchioles

lung

alveolus

mucus | trapped dirt | beating cilia

paralyzed cilia

7

Smoke and fumes

Bronchitis is a lung disease which is closely related to the amount of pollution in the air we breathe. As the amount of smoke in the air is reduced, due to restrictions on burning smoky fuel, the number of deaths from bronchitis falls. In this diagram, you can see how the deaths from bronchitis in Great Britain fell as the air became cleaner, except for the winter of 1962–63, when there was a serious smog.

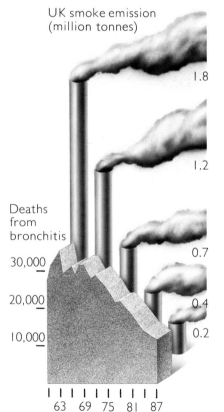

UK smoke emission (million tonnes)

1.8

1.2

0.7

Deaths from bronchitis

30,000

20,000

10,000

0.4

0.2

63 69 75 81 87

When fuels such as coal, oil and gasoline burn, they produce a whole range of gases, together with solid materials such as soot and tar particles which are a threat to health. When coal fires were widely used in homes, these materials frequently produced thick, evil-smelling, smoky fogs called "smog" which killed many people. In a four-day smog in London in 1952, there were 4,000 more deaths than normal. In most places, the use of smoky fuel is now forbidden.

Los Angeles, in California, is well known for its smog. This is produced when chemicals from car exhausts react with light. The thick haze that results can last for several days, causing breathing problems especially among old people.

Car exhausts and power stations produce sulfur dioxide and nitrogen oxides, gases which irritate the lungs, causing coughing and watering eyes. In large amounts they can cause permanent lung damage. Another product of burning oil or gasoline is carbon monoxide, which interferes with the body's proper use of oxygen.

Air pollution is a serious problem in many cities. It can be produced from factories and power stations, as well as from car exhausts.

Lead and asbestos

Lead can be a dangerous poison if enough gets into the body. It is particularly dangerous for children. Where lead is added to gasoline, it is blown out in car exhausts and can pollute the environment. This diagram shows the amounts of lead (in micrograms) in dust samples taken in the United Kingdom in 1983. In the United States and some other countries the use of leaded gasoline is now banned or strictly limited.

Lead and asbestos are two very common materials in our environment. Each is a risk to health.

Lead is used in many forms. It may be added to gasoline to help it burn more evenly and is then passed into the air from car exhausts. Where leaded gasoline is used, more than 90 per cent of the lead inhaled comes from car exhausts. There are large amounts of lead in city dust. In old homes, there may be lead water pipes and lead paint; neither of these is used in modern houses.

The body cannot easily get rid of any lead which it takes in, and this can

Lead levels in dust samples

Urban playground
486

Rural road
570

Urban road
1,188

Main road
1,900

Town center street
2,100

Garage
12,100

Car park
12,900

10

When asbestos fibers are breathed into the lungs, they can cause a lot of damage. Asbestos was once used as a heat-resistant material in buildings, but is now being removed. This workman wears a respirator to protect his lungs as he removes asbestos and packs its away into a sack.

In this photomicrograph, an asbestos fiber can be seen penetrating a cell from the lungs of a person suffering from the disease asbestosis.

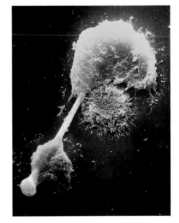

sometimes build up to become a serious health risk, especially in young children.

Asbestos is a gray, mineral, fireproof material used in buildings. When left strictly alone it is harmless, but if it is disturbed, tiny fibers are carried through the air and can settle in the lungs. Here they can cause scarring or **asbestosis**, and people regularly exposed to asbestos may suffer from a very dangerous form of **cancer**. The use of asbestos is now restricted by law and it is being removed from many buildings.

Disease and the working environment

Exposure to pollutants in the working environment can damage health.

Lung disease is a common hazard in many industries. Miners have been especially at risk from inhaling mineral dust. **Black lung** is a disease in which the lungs become blackened and hard, due to the amount of dust they contain. Woodworkers have been similarly affected by inhaling sawdust, and the lungs of workers in the cotton industry have been damaged by cotton fibers. In all these conditions, the normally flexible lung tissue is gradually replaced by hard, fibrous tissue that interferes with breathing and makes diseases such as bronchitis and **lung cancer** more likely. Workers now have to wear masks and respirators in dusty environments and special filters are added to machinery to reduce dust levels.

Contact with chemicals can cause skin problems such as **dermatitis**, and if the chemicals are absorbed through the skin, there may be more serious effects. It has been found, for example, that certain chemicals can cause cancer, and their use is now restricted. Protective clothing must be worn.

Dust from coal and other minerals often collects in the lungs of miners, and causes lung disease. In this photomicrograph, black deposits of coal dust can be seen in a miner's lung.

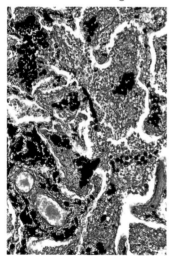

There are health risks with many occupations and regulations about the use of protective clothing are intended to make work safer. Most of these health hazards relate to inhaling dust or fumes, but contact with the skin can also be a health risk. For example, surgeons must be protected from contact with infected blood and tissue and florists can develop skin irritations through constant contact with certain types of flowering plants. Noise, too, can be damaging and in some occupations ear protectors are worn.

1 Nuclear power station worker
2 Painter
3 Florist
4 Nurse
5 Tractor driver
6 Miner
7 Fireman
8 Pigeon racer
9 Chimney cleaner
10 Welder

Industrial pollution

If industrial waste is not disposed of safely, the after-effects can take years to clear up.

Industrial waste is often dumped in special sites. These are usually old quarries which are then filled in to cover the waste and keep it harmless. But sometimes the waste containers leak, or chemicals are dumped illegally, and dangerous substances leak out and contaminate water supplies. In the United States, in the 1930s, chemicals were dumped into a ditch which was later built on. The effects were not noticed until the 1970s, when trees began to die, and the inhabitants suffered from nervous system and liver disorders.

Rivers like the Rhine, running through Europe's busiest industrial areas, are very vulnerable to toxic wastes. These wastes enter the food chain, affecting fish in the North Sea which people will eventually eat.

The pollution caused by industrial accidents can have very serious effects. Recent accidents at Seveso in Italy and Bhopal in India caused the release of toxic chemicals which will probably affect people's health for years to come.

Opposite
Industrial pollution has been responsible for some great environmental disasters. When a chemical plant at Bhopal in India exploded, the huge cloud of poisonous fumes it released affected thousands of people. Many died and still more were blinded by the effects of the fumes.

Cigarettes and passive smoking

Nearly everyone now accepts that cigarette smoking greatly increases the risk of bronchitis, lung cancer or heart disease. But many adults continue to smoke, and many young people pick up the habit.

Unfortunately, cigarette smoking not only affects the smoker, it damages the environment and the health of other people too. Just being in a smoky room is the equivalent of smoking one

There is now no doubt that exposure to other people's cigarette smoke is damaging to health. For non-smokers who work in smoky environments, lung cancer is more common than would normally be expected. Children whose parents smoke are more likely to suffer from coughs and respiratory diseases.

Respiratory illness 5–9 years

Persistent cough 8–19 years

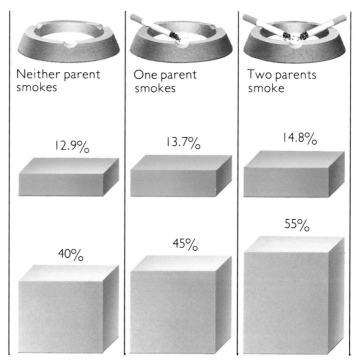

Neither parent smokes

One parent smokes

Two parents smoke

12.9%

13.7%

14.8%

40%

45%

55%

The risk seems to be greatest for the families of smokers and young people are more likely to suffer lung problems if their parents smoke. It is known that the non-smoking wives of male smokers are about a third more likely to develop lung cancer than the non-smoking wives of non-smokers. The smoke drifting from another person's cigarette contains a much worse mixture of damaging chemicals than the smoke the smoker inhales – five times as much carbon monoxide, which can be harmful to the heart and circulation and about fifty times as much of the cancer-causing chemicals.

Many smokers are just becoming aware of the irritation their habit can cause to non-smokers. Children who grow up in a smoky environment can suffer respiratory damage at an early age.

Pure water?

Probably the biggest single factor in improving health during the past century has been the introduction of "safe" drinking water. But in many countries, infections from contaminated drinking water still cause deaths, as well as an enormous amount of sickness and loss of productivity.

One of the most important elements in providing safe water is to prevent contamination of the rivers with sewage, a major cause of serious stomach and intestinal infections. Modern sewage treatment plants can remove all health

Pure drinking water is essential for health. To make sure that the water we drink is pure, and stays pure, constant monitoring is necessary. This ensures that no dangerous micro-organisms escape the purification process and that no unwanted substances, contaminate the water.

18

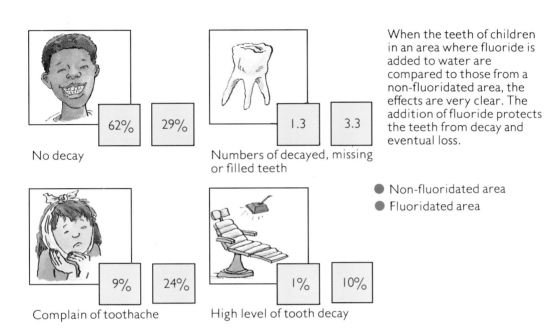

No decay 62% 29%

Numbers of decayed, missing or filled teeth 1.3 3.3

Complain of toothache 9% 24%

High level of tooth decay 1% 10%

When the teeth of children in an area where fluoride is added to water are compared to those from a non-fluoridated area, the effects are very clear. The addition of fluoride protects the teeth from decay and eventual loss.

● Non-fluoridated area
● Fluoridated area

risks from treated water. Chlorine is added to drinking water in small amounts, to kill any organisms. Bottled water is safe because it has been filtered through many layers of rock.

In many areas, **fluoride** is added to drinking water in tiny amounts, to protect the teeth from decay. Sometimes fluoride is found naturally in water supplies, and it was the discovery that children in these areas had very healthy teeth that led to the addition of fluoride to water supplies in other areas.

What else are we drinking?

Farm chemicals applied to crops by a crop sprayer can be washed out of the air and the soil and into our drinking water supply.

Most of the rain that falls on land soaks down through the soil and eventually reaches the rivers or enters the water table – a layer of water deep below us, often used as the source of water from wells. Water carries with it any pollutants absorbed from the air, together with substances washed out of the soil.

Many chemicals get into water supplies as a result of industry and

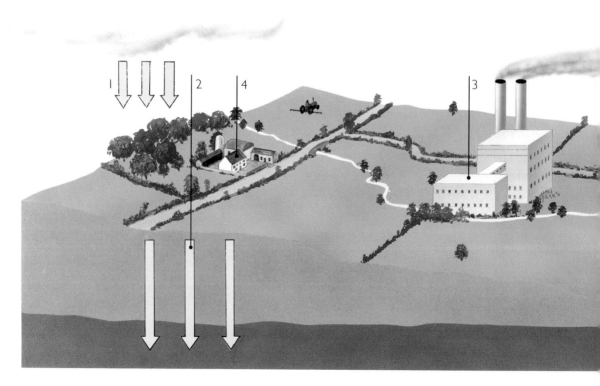

because of modern farming practices which depend heavily on the use of chemical fertilizers and pesticides. Modern agriculture needs large amounts of nitrogen to stimulate rapid crop growth. Much of the excess nitrogen is washed into drinking water supplies and, in some areas, has reached levels which are considered to be dangerous to babies. There is also concern about a cancer risk due to **nitrates** being broken down in the body.

Pollutants reach our water supply in several ways.

1 Rainfall washes chemicals into the soil.
2 Fertilizers drain into the water table.
3 Air pollution from factories.
4 Domestic air pollution.
5 Rainfall traps airborne pollutants.
6 More waste drains from industrial dumping.
7 Drinking water pumped from rivers.
8 Drinking water pumped from wells.
9 Water purification plant.

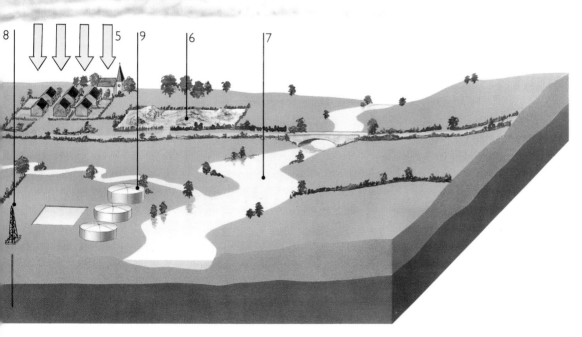

Do you know what you're eating?

Although the food you eat may look, taste and smell fresh and inviting, it may contain a number of **additives**, put in for several different reasons.

Food must look attractive if people are to buy it, so the food manufacturers often add coloring to restore color lost during the cooking process. Other substances improve the texture of foods, or help them stay fresh for longer.

There is concern about certain types of additive which may be a risk to health. A few children react against certain food colorings, and may have behavioral disorders. This has led to concern about other types of additives such as preservatives. But, on the whole, the addition of preservatives, especially to meat products, is worthwhile, because they reduce the risk of contamination with food-poisoning bacteria.

Some additives are put into foods simply to replace essential substances like vitamins which are lost in the cooking process. In some countries, there are regulations stating the exact amount of **nutrients** that must be present in foods such as bread, which may form a large part of the diet.

What's in a hot dog? It appears to contain meat, bread and relish. But often familiar foods are not quite what they seem. Below, you will find a list of the typical ingredients of a hot dog, its bread and relishes. These are listed in order, according to the amount present.

Bread roll:
Flour
Water
Invert sugar
Yeast
Hydrogenated vegetable oil
Salt
Emulsifier, mono- and di-acetyltartaric acid esters of mono- and di-glycerides of fatty acids
Soya flour
Dextrose
Flour "improvers" – L-Ascorbic acid, potassium bromate, chlorine dioxide

Frankfurter:
Beef and chicken (including ground bone and gristle, and up to 30% fat)
Water
Starch
Salt
Caseinate (milk protein)
Soya protein
Sugar
Spices
Sodium polyphosphate
Antioxidant, sodium L-Ascorbate
Preservative, sodium nitrite

Ketchup:
Tomato
Water
Sugar
Acetic acid
Salt
Spices
Onion extract
Thickener, Xanthan gum
Color, caramel
Vegetable protein
Flavoring

Mustard
Mustard
Water
Sugar
Salt
Wheat flour
Malic acid
Colors – titanium dioxide, tartrazine
Stabilizer, Xanthan gum

Relish
Tomato
Sugar
Onions
Gherkins
Pimentos
Acetic acid
Starch
Spices
Malt extract
Mustard
Thickener, Guar gum
Preservative, potassium sorbate

Unwanted additions to our diet

Fruit and vegetables are no longer restricted to a particular season, because they can be shipped from other countries or stored for long periods. Chemicals are often sprayed on fruit and vegetables at the time of harvesting to prevent decay. Traces of these chemicals may be present on food bought weeks or months later. Fertilizers and pesticides are also used on fruit and vegetables to prevent the growth of molds and fungi which could be dangerous to health. Traces of these may also remain, but in the amounts used, should not be dangerous.

Modern, livestock farming depends on rearing animals very quickly, so that they do not consume too much food. In many areas, they are given **hormones** or other substances to make them grow rapidly, and some people are concerned that small amounts of these materials may remain in meat or eggs. **Antibiotic** drugs are also given to prevent illness caused by infections. These have caused serious problems in some countries where animal bacteria have resisted the drugs and caused outbreaks of disease in humans.

To prevent disease, modern poultry farmers give their birds drugs every day. Other drugs make them grow faster, so they are cheaper to rear. Some of these chemicals can remain in the chickens we eat, or in their eggs.

It's difficult to think of any food "healthier" than an apple. But the apple on the right has been held over steam for a few minutes, making the wax coating it has been given become visible. The coating makes the fruit look more attractive. But it may also contain preservatives or fungicides, which we eat along with the apple.

The end of the food chain

When 600 tons of mercury were dumped into the sea from a factory near the Japanese village of Minamata, no one knew it would cause paralysis and even death for many people. The mercury entered the food chain and poisoned villagers who ate the fish they caught. This 16-year-old girl was damaged by mercury while still in her mother's womb.

All living organisms are interlinked in a process called the food chain. Small organisms are eaten by larger ones, and these in turn are eaten by still larger animals, until the food chain reaches us. The whole process starts with bacteria and microscopic plants, which feed by absorbing chemicals from the environment. They in turn are food for other small creatures. When larger creatures eat these small organisms, they also take in the substances they contain. The amount of chemicals gradually increases at each stage in the chain.

Microscopic plants absorb chemicals in the water.

Tiny animals in the plankton feed on microscopic plants.

Shrimp and small fish eat smaller organisms, concentrating the contaminants.

Levels in mackerel and other fish may be dangerous to humans.

Mercury and other substances enter the food chain. The amounts of these substances gradually increase at each stage. By the time we eat fish, there may be large amounts of contaminants present.

Eventually, the level of harmful chemicals ingested can be dangerous.

Large amounts of mercury, a poisonous metal, were discharged into the sea from an industrial plant in Japan and entered the food chain. Eventually, the mercury became concentrated in mackerel, which were eaten by Japanese fishermen and villagers. Many of these people suffered brain damage or became paralyzed as a result of mercury poisoning. This became known as **minamata disease**, after the village most affected.

Radiation all around us

Radiation is a term used to describe a form of energy which affects all of us and which, under some circumstances, can be harmful.

Radiation is present in the ground, in buildings, food and drink, and in the air we breathe. In some parts of the world, where granite rock lies just beneath the surface, radioactive **radon gas** leaks out of the rock and can collect in sealed rooms and cellars. There is concern that this can cause dangerous radiation levels.

Microwaves are a form of non-ionizing radiation which can be used for cooking. Much more powerful microwaves are used for communication, sending messages in narrow, concentrated beams over great distances between towers like this, which are linked to the telephone system.

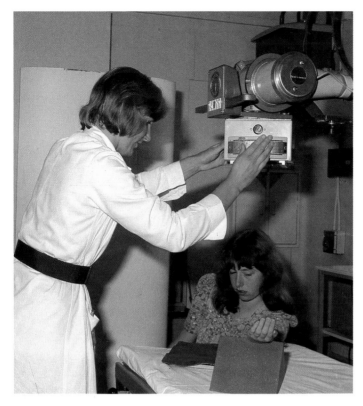

X-rays are a powerful form of ionizing radiation, used to photograph the interior of the body to help diagnose disease or damage. Exposure to X-rays must be brief, to avoid injuring the tissues, as a result, operators take special precautions to protect themselves and their patients from the effects.

The form of radiation which causes most concern is known as "ionizing radiation," and this is the type that can damage cells and threaten health. But most of this radiation is perfectly natural. Eighty-seven per cent of the radiation we experience comes from natural sources; only 13 per cent is man-made.

X-rays are a form of radiation which do have an element of risk, if over-used. Medical X-rays are carefully controlled, and there is little risk for the person being X-rayed. The real danger is for the operator of the equipment, who needs to take special precautions to avoid radiation damage.

29

The threat from nuclear radiation

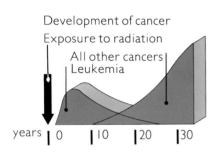

Development of cancer
Exposure to radiation
All other cancers
Leukemia

years | 0 | 10 | 20 | 30

Exposure to radiation can cause cancer, which may take many years to develop. Leukemia, a blood cancer, develops more quickly. When several cases of leukemia occur unexpectedly near a nuclear power station, it could mean that other forms of cancer will develop later.

The threat of nuclear war has been with us for more than forty years, but for many people, the risk of accidental nuclear disaster is more worrying. Nuclear power stations are now common, and offer economical electric power without smoke and fumes. However, the consequences of an accident at one of these power stations are very serious, as has been shown by three major accidents in recent years, at Three Mile Island in the United States, Sellafield in the UK and Chernobyl in the USSR. After the accident at Chernobyl, radiation got into the food chain in Lapland and built up to levels which made reindeer dangerous to eat.

Some people died immediately following the Chernobyl accident; many more may be affected over the years to come. It takes a long time for the full effects of radiation to be seen. Cancer is the main threat, and it has been found that **leukemia**, a form of cancer of the blood, is more common than usual around the site of the nuclear accident at Sellafield, and very common at Hiroshima and Nagasaki, where the first atomic bombs were dropped.

Because of fears about the danger of transporting nuclear waste by train, this old locomotive was deliberately crashed into the yellow nuclear waste container to see if it could withstand the impact. The container did not leak.

Too much sun?

Chlorofluorocarbons, substances found in aerosol cans, are now believed to damage the ozone layer in the upper atmosphere. They are being phased out and replaced with less harmful substitutes.

The ozone layer filters out the harmful effects of ultraviolet radiation in the sun's rays. But scientists have recently discovered a huge hole in the ozone layer, probably caused by chlorofluorocarbons. Ultraviolet can now pass through this hole without hindrance.

The sun's rays contain **ultraviolet** light, the form of radiation which causes the skin to tan. But ultraviolet light can be damaging. Sunburn, for example, is caused by overexposure to ultraviolet light. Too much sun, can also cause more serious damage. White people living in hot climates often suffer permanent skin damage from too much sun and some develop skin cancer.

Ultraviolet rays are normally prevented from doing too much damage by a layer of ozone gas, high above the atmosphere which acts as a filter. But fears that substances called **chlorofluorocarbons**, used as propellants in aerosol cans, can build up

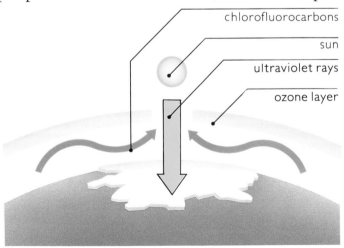

chlorofluorocarbons

sun

ultraviolet rays

ozone layer

Although many people like to sunbathe, overexposure to ultraviolet rays in sunlight can cause skin damage, and may lead to skin cancer.

In the thin upper air, mountaineers are exposed to high levels of ultraviolet radiation, and must take precautions against sunburn.

and damage the **ozone layer** have recently been confirmed. An enormous hole in the ozone layer has been discovered over the Antarctic, and this is allowing ultraviolet to pass through without hindrance. If the ozone layer continues to break down, this could mean an increase in skin cancers in years to come, especially in fair-skinned people.

Ultraviolet is also filtered as it passes through the air, and at high altitudes, its burning effects are much stronger. This is why, even though it is cold, it is possible to become badly sunburned while skiing.

Problems with the temperature

Humans can cope with a remarkable range of temperatures and can survive happily in the coldest climates, provided warm clothing is worn.

Opposite
Protection from the sun is important in tropical climates. This Samoan policeman wears an adaptation of local dress which keeps him cool, while he is shaded from direct sunlight.

Humans function properly only within a narrow range of temperatures. If it is too hot or too cold, we need special protection from the effects.

We can adjust to living in very high temperatures, but it takes weeks for the body to adapt fully. Living and working in hot climates means avoiding the sun at the hottest times of day, resting more often, and drinking large amounts of liquid to replace that lost by sweating. People vacationing in hot climates, often fail to allow time for adjustment, and suffer sunburn and **heat stroke** as a result.

The effects of cold are just as dangerous as heat, especially for the elderly. Old people do not have good control of their body temperature, and are often not aware that they are becoming dangerously cold. Unfortunately, as the body becomes chilled, the senses become less efficient. Old people affected by cold, or people caught out in the open in very cold weather, often fail to take the right action to protect themselves from harm. This may result in **hypothermia** which, if not treated promptly, can cause death.

Noise and health

If used at too high a volume, personal stereos can cause severe hearing loss. Although the speakers are so tiny that they can even be fitted inside the ear, the sound they produce is directed straight down the ear canal and can cause damage if the volume is turned too high.

Noise is a form of pollution which can be merely irritating, or cause physical or emotional damage. For some people, the sound of music played very loudly is annoying, while others revel in it. Similarly, it may be enjoyable for some to drive a motor bike, while other people find the noise anti-social.

Long-term exposure to loud noise can bring about stress which has physical signs such as an increase in oxygen consumption and heart rate, possibly leading to effects on the heart and circulation. Tiredness, irritability and sleep disturbances may also occur.

The physical effects of noise on the ear can be serious. Prolonged, loud noise causes physical discomfort; it actually "hurts the ears." And if it is too loud or goes on for too long, it, at first, causes temporary hearing loss, then deafness, due to permanent damage to the delicate mechanism of the inner ear. Rock musicians performing in front of very powerful amplifiers frequently have permanent hearing damage. Even personal stereos can damage hearing, because all their sound output is directed straight into the ear.

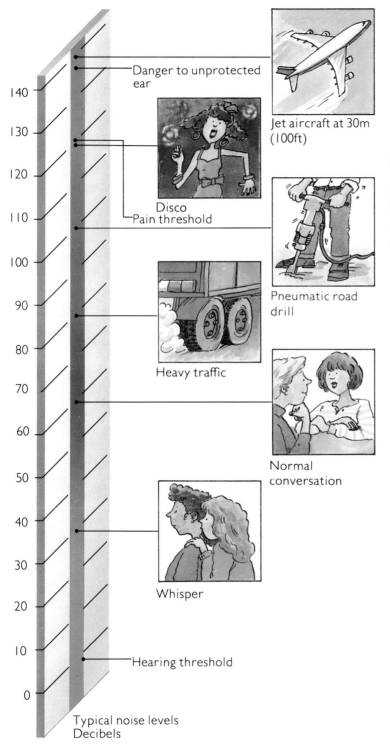

140

130

120

110

100

90

80

70

60

50

40

30

20

10

0

Danger to unprotected ear

Jet aircraft at 30m (100ft)

Disco
Pain threshold

Pneumatic road drill

Heavy traffic

Normal conversation

Whisper

Hearing threshold

Typical noise levels
Decibels

Excessive noise can have a serious effect on health and is associated with stress and anxiety. Very loud noise causes physical damage to the delicate structures in the ear and may result in deafness.

37

Stress at work

The work environment is a place where individuals are frequently under stress. There is pressure to succeed at school and in business, particularly in countries such as the United States and Japan. In this sort of environment, many people work long hours without taking time to relax, and both mental and physical stress are the result. We are also put under pressure to achieve certain lifestyles. Advertisements tell us that we must always have a better car or a bigger house if we are to succeed in life. In practice, most of us find we cannot achieve the lifestyle we are told we should like, so we become frustrated and stressed.

The pressure to conform with colleagues or friends is very strong. Certain professions, such as medicine and journalism, are well known as being likely to cause stress which can affect health. Alcohol abuse and **peptic ulcers** are common stress-related illnesses. The results of continuous stress are hard to measure, but they almost certainly increase the risk of heart attacks and emotional problems like anxiety and depression.

Opposite
Modern business methods have freed people from many routine and boring tasks, but have introduced new threats to health. These workers on the Hong Kong Stock Exchange work throughout the day at their computer terminals, under very stressful conditions. Headaches, backaches and anxiety are very common.

Deprivation and ill health

Ill health is a constant threat to the deprived or disadvantaged. Poor diet and overcrowding lead to stress and increase the risk of infection. Emotional problems such as depression and anxiety are common, especially when housing conditions are bad, and where people are unemployed or have low incomes.

For the elderly, who often have to live on restricted incomes, heating bills and the cost of food are important influences on health. Diseases such as arthritis are not caused by cold or deprivation, but their effects are much worse under these conditions. **Pneumonia** is a threat to old people whose resistance is low because of self-neglect.

People living in many of the tower blocks built in the 1960s suffer from anxiety and stress. The blocks are now deteriorating and vandalized, and this contributes to the poor quality of life for the occupants.

Nearly all large cities contain slums which house the poorest members of society. In these conditions, there is a high rate of infant mortality and many children are poorly nourished.

Public welfare programs and free health care all contribute toward improving the health of deprived people. It has been found that quite small improvements in sanitation, water supplies, diet and home heating can provide great health benefits. Improvements in living standards meant that diseases like **diptheria** and **tuberculosis** started to disappear before vaccination began.

Accidents and safety

Most accidents are preventable and are caused by carelessness or thoughtlessness.

Many more accidents happen in the home than on the highways. Fires are particularly dangerous and cause much loss of life and injury. Fires in upholstered furniture are the most serious. They give off clouds of black, choking, poisonous smoke that can kill sleeping people within just a few minutes. With anything but a very small fire, get out of the house fast!

Babies are particularly at risk in the home, because they lack the experience to know when they are in a dangerous situation. Many babies are burned or poisoned because their parents overlook the risks.

Most accidents are minor, caused by cuts, falls, burns and scalds. Although all of these are easily prevented, you must recognize that it is impossible to make your home, school or place of work totally safe, We all depend on common sense to prevent accidents. This is why it is so important to be careful with young children, who do not have the experience to know when they are in danger. Elderly people too can sometimes put themselves at risk, especially on the road. Failing sight or poor hearing may make them unaware that a car or motor bike is coming.

The roads are very dangerous places for unsupervised play. Even the most careful driver cannot avoid a child who suddenly moves into the road, right in front of the car.

Useful addresses

American Cancer Society
777 Third Avenue
New York, New York 10017

**American Lung
Association**
1740 Broadway
New York, New York 10019

**Citizens Clearinghouse
for Hazardous Wastes**
P.O. Box 926
Arlington, Virginia 22216

Clean Coal Coalition
1828 L Street, N.W.
Washington, D.C. 20036

**Clean Water Action
Project**
317 Pennsylvania Avenue,
S.E.
Washington, D.C. 20003

**Coalition for a National
Health Service**
P.O. Box 6586
T Street Station
Washington, D.C. 20009

**Committee for National
Health Insurance**
1757 N Street, N.W.
Washington, D.C. 20036

**Consumer Product Safety
Commission**
1111 Eighteenth Street,
N.W.
Washington, D.C. 20207

**The Department of
Energy**
Washington, D.C. 20585

**Environmental Action
Foundation**
1525 New Hampshire
Avenue, N.W.
Washington, D.C. 20036

**Environmental Data and
Information Service**
3300 Whitehaven Street,
N.W.
Washington, D.C. 20007

**Environmental Defense
Fund**
1616 P Street, N.W.
Washington, D.C. 20036

**Food Safety and Quality
Service**
Department of Agriculture
Fourteenth Street and
Independence Avenue, S.W.
Washington, D.C. 20250

Greenpeace, U.S.A.
1611 Connecticut Avenue,
N.W.
Washington D.C. 20009

**International Society for
Flouride Research**
P.O. Box 692
Warren, Michigan 48090

**National Clear Air
Coalition**
530 Seventh Street, S.E.
Washington, D.C. 20003

**National Council of the
Paper Industry for Air
and Stream
Improvement, Inc.**
260 Madison Avenue
New York, New York 10016

**United States
Environmental
Protection Agency**
Washington, D.C. 20460

**Water Pollution Control
Federation**
2626 Pennsylvania Avenue
Washington, D.C. 20037

Glossary

Additives: substances added to food in order to change or protect it.

Alveolus: tiny, bladder-like structure in the lung, with a thin wall through which oxygen and carbon dioxide pass freely. The lungs contain millions of alveoli.

Antibiotic a substance which kills or damages bacteria, so the body's natural defences can destroy them.

Arthritis: disease which affects joints, making them swollen and painful.

Asbestosis: a lung disease caused by exposure to fibres from asbestos, a mineral substance commonly used as a fire-proof material in buildings.

Black lung: disease caused by inhaling mineral dust which makes the lungs hard and stony, so that it becomes difficult to breathe.

Bronchi: large, reinforced tubes which carry air into and out of the lungs.

Bronchioles: the smallest air tubes in the lungs, carrying air to and from the alveoli.

Bronchitis: disease in which the walls of the bronchi become inflamed and swollen. Bronchitis can be caused or made worse by breathing polluted air (such as inhaling cigarette smoke).

Cancer: disease in which body cells reproduce uncontrollably and, unless treated properly, may spread through the body.

Chlorofluorocarbons: substances which are used as propellants, to drive out the contents in aerosol cans. They are believed to have caused severe damage to the ozone layer.

Cilia: tiny hairs which beat back and forth, causing a current in the liquid mucus covering them.

Dermatitis: condition in which the skin becomes sore and inflamed, often because of frequent contact with an irritant substance.

Diphtheria: very severe throat infection which was once very common among children. Now prevented by vaccination.

Fluoride: substance which can be absorbed into the teeth of young people, making them very hard and resistant to decay.

Hay fever: allergic disease caused when the body reacts strongly against inhaled pollen.

Heat stroke: dangerous condition in which the body's normal cooling system fails. It usually happens after very vigorous exertion in extremely hot weather, when the body produces heat faster than it can be lost to the air.

Hormones: substance carried in the blood, which can affect or control the function of organs or tissues.

Hypothermia: cooling of the body temperature to a point where the organs no longer work properly.

Leukemia: form of cancer affecting white blood cells, which are present in very large numbers, but do not function properly.

Lung cancer: type of cancer which first attacks the lungs, then may spread to other parts of the body.

Minamata disease: disease caused by eating food contaminated with toxic metals such as mercury. It was first noticed in Japan, where it affected people who had eaten fish contaminated with industrial waste.

Mucus: sticky, watery liquid which lubricates and protects many parts of the body.

Nitrates: substances used in chemical fertilizers, which can be washed into water supplies. Nitrates can be dangerous if they are present in large amounts.

Nutrient: food substance which is used to supply energy for the body, or to help build new body cells.

Ozone layer: layer of the colourless gas, ozone, which surrounds the world high in the atmosphere. The ozone layer filters out much of the sun's ultraviolet radiation.

Peptic ulcer: painful damage to the stomach wall, which may be associated with continual stress and anxiety.

Pneumonia: infection in which the lungs fill with fluid, interfering with breathing.

Radon gas: radioactive gas which leaks out of the ground in very small amounts, in areas where certain types of rock are near to the surface. Where radon collects in houses, it is thought there may be a health risk.

Radiation: a type of energy. The term is usually used to describe the energy given off by radioactive substances such as radium, uranium and plutonium. Radiation can sometimes be used medically to treat or diagnose disease, but is dangerous in large amounts.

Respirator: device worn over the nose and mouth to purify air before it is inhaled.

Trachea: large reinforced tube at the back of the throat, carrying air to the lungs via the bronchi.

Tuberculosis: infectious disease which often attacks the lungs. It is now uncommon, because most children are vaccinated against it.

Ultraviolet rays: type of radiation present in sunlight. In small amounts it is harmless, but long exposure causes painful sunburn and, in extreme cases, may lead to skin cancer.

X-ray: form of radiation used for medical diagnosis. X-rays penetrate the body and can be used to produce a ''picture'' of internal structures such as bones.

Index

PRINTED IN BELGIUM BY

proost
INTERNATIONAL BOOK PRODUCTION